The Music Of Mark Sherman

First Edition

Created By Sandra Forchetti
For Miles High Records

Copyrights © 2011 by Shermark Music.
All rights reserved. No part of this book may be reproduced or transmitted, in any form or by any means, including recording or photocopied, without prior written permission of the author, except in the case of brief quotations embodied in critical articles and reviews.

Credits

Project Manager: Sandra Forchetti
Cover Photo, and photos on page 34,49, 53 by Chris Drukker
Produced by Sandra Forchetti for Miles High Records

My deepest thanks and appreciation to all the musicians, and friends listed below who have brought many of these tunes to life with their individual mastery, and craft in the art form we pursue. Through my many recordings, and tours these tunes have grown a life of their own.

Allen Farnham, Dean Johnson, Tim Horner, Joe Magnarelli, Rodney Jones, Larry Coryell, Michael Brecker, Joe Lovano, Randy Brecker, Jerry Bergonzi, Lonnie Plaxico, Buster Williams, Joe Locke, Eric Harland, Jim Ridl, Tom DiCarlo, Chembo Corniel, Jeremy Manasia, Paul Wickliffe, David Chesky, Larry Robbins, Sandra Forchetti, Paul Rice, Miles Sherman, Roger Robindore', Bob Clearmountain, and Apogee Electronics, Mark Elf, Ann Braithwaite, Alejandro Orellano, Antonio Soriano, Chris Drukker, Kathy Ridl, Antonio Merola, and anyone else I may have left out. THANK YOU!

ISBN 978-0615568713

www.mileshighrecords.com
Music information site: www.markshermanmusic.com

Contents

Introduction .... page 6
Biography .... page 8
Discography .... page 10
Teaching Philosophy .... page 13

Motive Series
Motive # 10 Judaican (for Kenny Kirkland) .... page 16
Motive # 1 .... page 18
Motive # 11 Always Reaching .... page 20
Motive # 7 Alla Sandra .... page 22
Motive # 3 That Moment .... page 25
Motive # 4 Venture Within .... page 26
Motive # 9 Soothing Dream .... page 28
Motive # 8 Altered .... page 30

One Step Closer
Modal Blues .... page 35
Little Lullaby .... page 36
Spiritual Exercise .... page 38
Ella Bella .... page 41
My Princess .... page 42
Long Trip Home .... page 44

Family First
Explorations .... page 50
Fantasize .... page 54
Family First .... page 56
With Hope .... page 58
Symmetrical .... page 60

Live @ The Bird's Eye
Tip Top Blues .... page 63
The Winning Life .... page 64
Trust .... page 66
Tip Top Rhythm .... page 67
Hardship .... page 68

Good Rhythm Good Vibes / Live @ Sweet Rhythm NYC (DVD)
The Great Trip(let) .... page 72
Sandy .... page 74
Gift For A Friend .... page 76
Beautiful Girl .... page 78

Live @ Chorus Jazz Club
With Soul From Seoul .... page 81
Primitive Reality .... page 82
Solitude .... page 84
My Warm Heart .... page 86
Tree Of Life .... page 88

Introduction

After around 35 years touring the world professionally in the many areas of music as both a sideman, and a leader, I am very proud to finally publish some of my original compositions. For many years people have asked me about my different originals, as well as enquire about the availability of the lead sheets. Finally, I have assembled them into a book format. The book begins chronologically from 2003- 2011. My last 6 projects as a leader starting with the *"The Motive Series", "One Step Closer", "Family First", "Live At The Bird's Eye", "Good Rhythms Good Vibes"*, and *"Live at Chorus Jazz Club"*. You will surely notice how my harmonic language skills grow and change over the years. Feel free to explore the different ways these tunes can be performed. Many can be played in multiple styles, and you can just use the harmonic/rhythmic roadmap, and melody your way. In addition, you will see a few brief educational concepts in my teaching philosophy that I live, as well as pass on to my many students globally.

I hope you enjoy the music!

About Mark Sherman

Biography

After nearly 30 years of recording, composing, and performing with countless orchestras, jazz artists, and vocal artists, vibraphonist/composer Mark Sherman is a Yamaha performing artist, Pro Mark artist, and a *Winner of Rising Star Vibes 2007-2010 in Down Beat magazine critics poll*. Sherman's recording in 2005 ***"The Motive Series"*** featuring the late Michael Brecker, and the 2006 recording ***"One Step Closer"*** featuring Joe Lovano both received overwhelming response on the jazz radio charts for 14 weeks in the United States with ***"One Step Closer"*** peaking in the top ten on the charts. His recording in 2007 ***"Family First"*** was the most spun CD in the United States in it's opening week on the charts, and his recording done live at the Bird's Eye Jazz Club in Basel, Switzerland at the close of a 2 week European tour (2008), is entitled *Mark Sherman Quartet* ***"Live at The Bird's Eye"*** and continues to get rave reviews and big radio response. Mark's most recent recordings are a live filming for DVD entitled ***"Live At Sweet Rhythm NYC"*** of his quintet featuring his band of 7 years with Joe Magnarelli, Allen Farnham, Dean Johnson, and Tim Horner. ***"The LA Sessions"*** an organ trio recording of bebop, and standards featuring Bill Cunliffe, Charles Ruggiero, and John Chiodini, and Mark Sherman Quartet ***"Live At Chorus Jazz Club"*** is due out in April 2012

Tied in with most of Sherman's live performances (clubs, and festivals) is a 2 hour master-class on language skills for improvisation, usually done at the local music school or university music department, and sponsored by Yamaha Corporation, and Pro Mark. "These master-classes have been extremely successful at the high school and college level. I've received countless emails from students telling me how my system for learning the harmonic language needed for playing jazz was the simplest and most user friendly system they've come across, and that it answered many of the confusing questions, and got them improvising on chord changes very quickly."

Mark Sherman's background, Juilliard education, and working, performance and recording experience have all contributed to a unique vision, which incorporates elements of jazz, blues, and classical music. Accomplished as a soloist (vibraphone/piano/drums), ensemble player, composer, and educator, Sherman is in love with music and the re-harmonization of chords to explore and give expression to his musical vision.

The Bronx-born and raised son of a star soprano who performed with the Cleveland and Boston Symphony Orchestras had 5 years of classical piano lessons before he fell in love with jazz through Lester Young, Charlie Parker and John Coltrane LP's. After getting hooked on Elvin Jones, Mark sought him out as a teacher. What he learned most from Elvin was a feeling of "loose but intense swing" and how to "channel spiritual energy into music."

Sherman graduated from the High school of Music and Art under the guidance of Justin DiCiccio, and then went on to The Juilliard School, where he had 5 solid years of percussion training with tympani master Saul Goodman, and percussion master Elden (Buster) Bailey. He played in symphonic situations led by Zubin Mehta, Sir George Solti, and Leonard Bernstein, and many other fine conductors. At Juilliard he met another soul at home in both classical and jazz worlds Wynton Marsalis. They jammed together regularly and years later when Columbia Records George Butler inquired about Mark, Wynton's endorsement helped pave the way for Sherman's first major label record date A New Balance (CBS 1986). The single from that recording entitled "Changes In My Life" went double platinum in the Asia, and currently has over 6 million views on you tube.

Sherman toured globally with singers Jackie and Roy (4 years), which led to his recording and touring with The Peggy Lee Quintet (7years). From her he had lessons in how to "turn a musical phrase" and "subtle time." Working with the special musicians Lee surrounded herself with (Mike Renzi, Jay Leonhart, Grady Tate, and Jon Chiodini) led to gigs with Mel Torme, and recordings with other great artists including Maureen McGovern, Liza Minelli, Tony Bennett, Lena Horne, Ruth Brown, Gloria Lynn, Jennifer Holiday, Laverne Butler, Joe Beck, Larry Coryell, Rodney Jones and many others.

Discography

As a leader

- "The LA Sessions", MHR, 2012
- "Live At Chorus Jazz Club", MHR, 2012
- "Explorations In Space And Time"
  Lennie White, Jamey Hadad, Mark Sherman, Chesky Records, 2011
- "Good Rhythm, Good Vibes", Mark Sherman/Tim Horner 4tet, MHR, 2010
- "Live At Sweet Rhythm NYC" DVD, MHR, 2010
- "Live At The Bird's Eye", MHR, 2008
- "Family First", MHR, 2007
- "One Step Closer", MHR, 2005
- "The Motive Series, MHR, 2004
- "Spiral Staircase", MHR, 1999
- "High Rollin", MHR, 1998
- "A New Balance", CBS, 1986
- "Fulcrum Point", UNIS, 1980

As a sideman

- Tim Horner "The Place We Feel Free", MHR, 2011
- Dan Block "From His World To Mine", MHR, 2011
- Eddie Mendenhall "Cosine meets Tangent", MHR, 2011
- Andy Farber Big Band, 2010
- Capathia Jenkins/ Louis Rosen, PS Classics, 2009
- "Manure" (Original Soundtrack), 2008
- Jennifer Holiday, 2008
- "The Last Mimzy" (Original Soundtrack), 2006
- Lena Horne "Seasons Of A Life", Blue Note, 2006
- "See What I Wanna See" (Broadway Cast Album), 2006
- "Failure To Launch" (Original Soundtrack), 2006
- "The Light And The Piazza" (Broadway Cast Album), 2005
- Cheryl Wheeler "Defying Gravity", CBS Masterworks, 2005
- "Last Holiday" (Original Soundtrack), 2005
- "Miss Congeniality" (Original Soundtrack), 2005
- Ann Hampton Callaway "Slow", Schanachie Records, 2004
- "The Alamo" (Original Soundtrack), 2004
- Ronnie Jordan "After 8", Blue Note, 2004
- "David Chesky's Surround Sound Show", 2004

- "Intolerable Cruelty" (Original Soundtrack), 2003
- DJ Spinna "Here To There", 2003
- Mary Fahl "The Other Side Of Time", CBS, 2003
- Blue Voices "The Finest In Jazz Ballads", 2003
- Liza Minelli "Liza's Back", 2002
- "Two Weeks Notice" (Original Soundtrack), 2002
- "The Rookie" (Original Soundtrack), 2002
- Ronnie Jordan "Off The Record", 2001
- "The Score" (Original Soundtrack), 2001
- Larry Coryell "New High", High Note, 2000
- Scott Hesse "Flame Within A Fire", 2000
- Rodney Jones "Undiscovered Few", Blue Note, 1999
- "Footloose" (Broadway Cast Album), 1999
- "Armagedeon", Aerosmith (Original Soundtrack), 1999
- Gloria Lynne "This One's On Me", High Note, 1998
- "The Lion King", Disney, 1998
- "Hercules", Disney (Original Soundtrack), 1998
- Michael Bolton "All That Matters", 1997
- Julian Coryell "Duality", N2K records, 1997
- "Steel Pier" (Original Cast Recording), 1997
- "Boys Next Door", 1996
- Larry Coryell "Sketches Of Coryell", Schanachie Records, 1996
- Chesky Records Collection #1, 1995
- Laverne Butler "No Lookin' Back", Chesky Records, 1994
- "Kiss Of The Spiderwoman" (Original Cast Recording), 1995
- "Rhymes and Fables" Cab Calloway, Freddie Hubbard, 1995
- Larry Coryell "I'll Be Over You", CTI Records, 1994 (Producer)
- "Best of Chesky Classics", Chesky Records, 1994
- Ruth Brown "Songs Of My Life", Fantasy Records, 1993
- Peggy Lee "Love Held Lightly Songs of Harold Arlen", 1993
- "Smooth Jazz Slow Jams", 1993
- "Christmas Songs Milestone", 1993
- Rodney Jones "The Unspoken Heart", 1992
- Laverne Butler "Daydreamin", Chesky Records, 1992
- "Love Songs", Sony, 1992
- Maureen Mcgovern, Gershwin CD, 1990
- Peggy Lee Songbook "There Will Never Be Another Spring", 1990
- Peggy Lee, Musicmasters, 1989
- "Peggy Lee Sings The Blues", 1989
- Maureen McGovern "Naughty Baby", CBS Masterworks, 1989
- Joe Beck, "Back To Beck", DMP records, 1988

Masterclass at The Seoul Jazz Academy, Korea 2010

Teaching Philosophy

"PRACTICE DOES NOT MAKE PERFECT! PERFECT PRACTICE MAKES PERFECT!"

My teaching philosophy is quite simple in theory.

I believe you must first learn to play your instrument focusing mainly on learning to get a good sound, and technique first through playing scales, and arpeggios, as well as long tones. Playing simple to difficult classical pieces can help you to develop your sound, phrasing, the use of legato, and staccato techniques, and the general interpretation of musical phrases. After this study as a foundation, playing jazz is much easier to learn and develop. So a strong classical background is important for beginners. You can then with your already developed technique on your instrument begin the quest to learn the rhythmic, and harmonic language skills, as well as the stylistic inflections needed to play jazz. In the study of jazz listening lists, and tune lists must be studied, as well as the drills used to improve your linear improvisations. And of course the most important piece of my philosophy is whatever you practice be sure to adhere to this concept. "PERFECT PRACTICE MAKES PERFECT"Practice method is everything. It will determine how fast one progresses. You must break passages down slowly, and repeat them slowly, and then increase speed little by little.

"I found Mark's teaching method to be the best I've yet encountered regarding what's REALLY important in jazz, i.e., his "triplets" concept re: feeling time,.... He knows how to convey all the essentials of extended harmony and at the same time keeps you glued to the basics of swinging, soulful phrasing plus how to listen & respond the other players. U can't get any better than that. (Larry Coryell)."

"Finally students of jazz improvisation have a clear guide in Mark Sherman. His method of integrating scales and chords into a linear and rhythmic framework is as satisfying and learning-friendly as I've seen. Any student of Mark's will immediately gain confidence, and the ability to play thru chord changes seamlessly. I applaud his enabling generosity.(Gordon Gottlieb-The Juilliard School)."

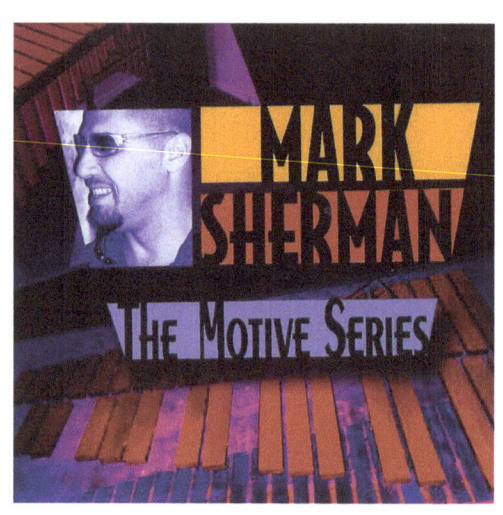

"I consider it no small honor to have been asked by Mark Sherman to write about him and his music. He has been an inspiring influence in my musical life for several years and I have learned a lot, sitting with him at the piano or standing at the vibes, getting a glimpse into how he negotiates harmony, writes a song, or voices a chord. I consider him to be one of the greatest vibraphonists of the post - Bobby Hutcherson / Mike Mainieri era. This is not to say that their time has come and gone. Hardly. They are both presently at the peak of their creative powers. It is simply that Mark is one of the few vibists in the generation to follow who got the entire message, and has the goods to pass it on. He has a beautiful sound, impeccable technique, and a mastery of the poetic language of jazz. I hear the voices of Bags and Bill Evans and Trane and McCoy, and so many, many more, all expressed through the medium of his mallets. As a fellow vibraphonist, I can only be grateful that Mark is around to offer his beautiful, and very personal take on this profound tradition. Aside from being a master of the instrument, he is, like Bobby and Mike, also a composer of formidable talent. His songs reveal a deep and soulful artist, ... "
(Joe Locke, New York City, June 2004).

For Kenny Kirkland featuring Michael Brecker

Motive #10 Judaican
"The Motive Series" CAP 980 2004

Mark Sherman

Motive #1

"The Motive Series" CAP 980 2004

Mark Sherman

Always Reaching

"The Motive Series" CAP 980 2004

Mark Sherman

Motive #7 Alla Sandra

"The Motive Series" CAP 980 2004

Waltz
Mark Sherman

SHERMARK MUSIC ASCAP

Motive #3 That Moment

Motive #4 Venture Within

"The Motive Series" CAP 980 2004

Mark Sherman

Motive #9 Soothing Dream

"The Motive Series" CAP 980 2004

Mark Sherman

Motive #8 Altered

"The Motive Series" CAP 980 2004

Mark Sherman

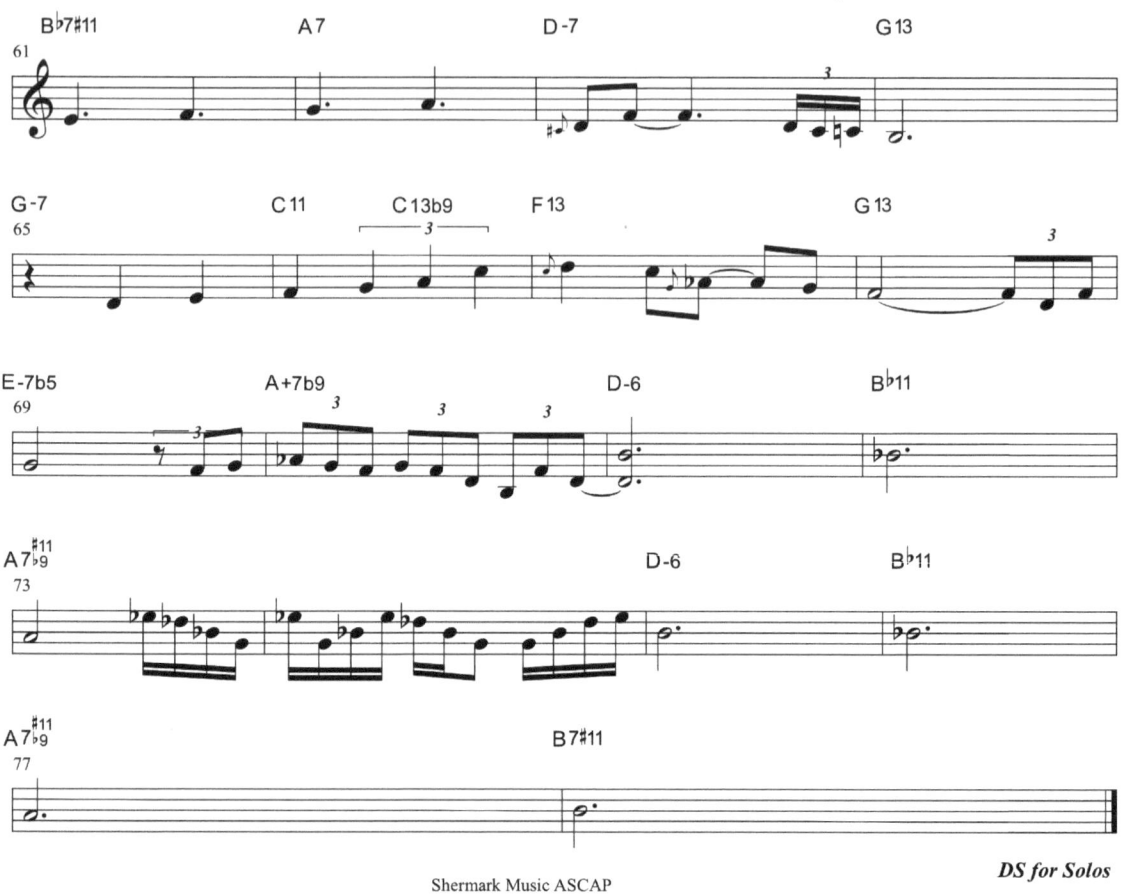

"I was really happy to be a part of this session with some of New York's most inspired and swinging musicians on today's scene… The music came alive from beat one and truly speaks for itself!!! (Joe Lovano)."

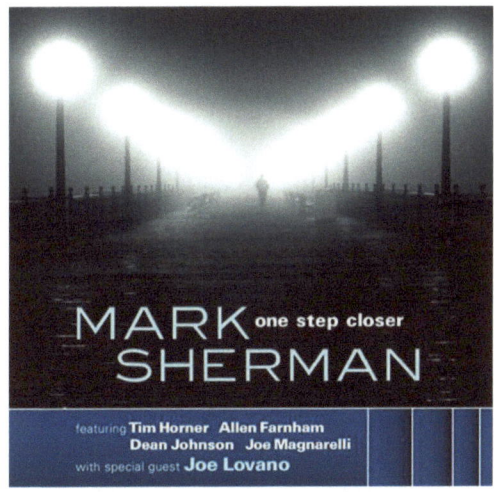

Modal Blues
"One Step Closer" CAP 991 2005

Mark Sherman

Shermark Music ASCAP

Little Lullaby
"One Step Closer" CAP 991 2005

Mark Sherman

Spiritual Excercise
"One Step Closer" CAp 991 2005

Mark Sherman

My Princess
"One Step Closer" CAP 991 2005

Mark Sherman

Long Trip Home
"One Step Closer" CAP 991 2005

Mark Sherman

45

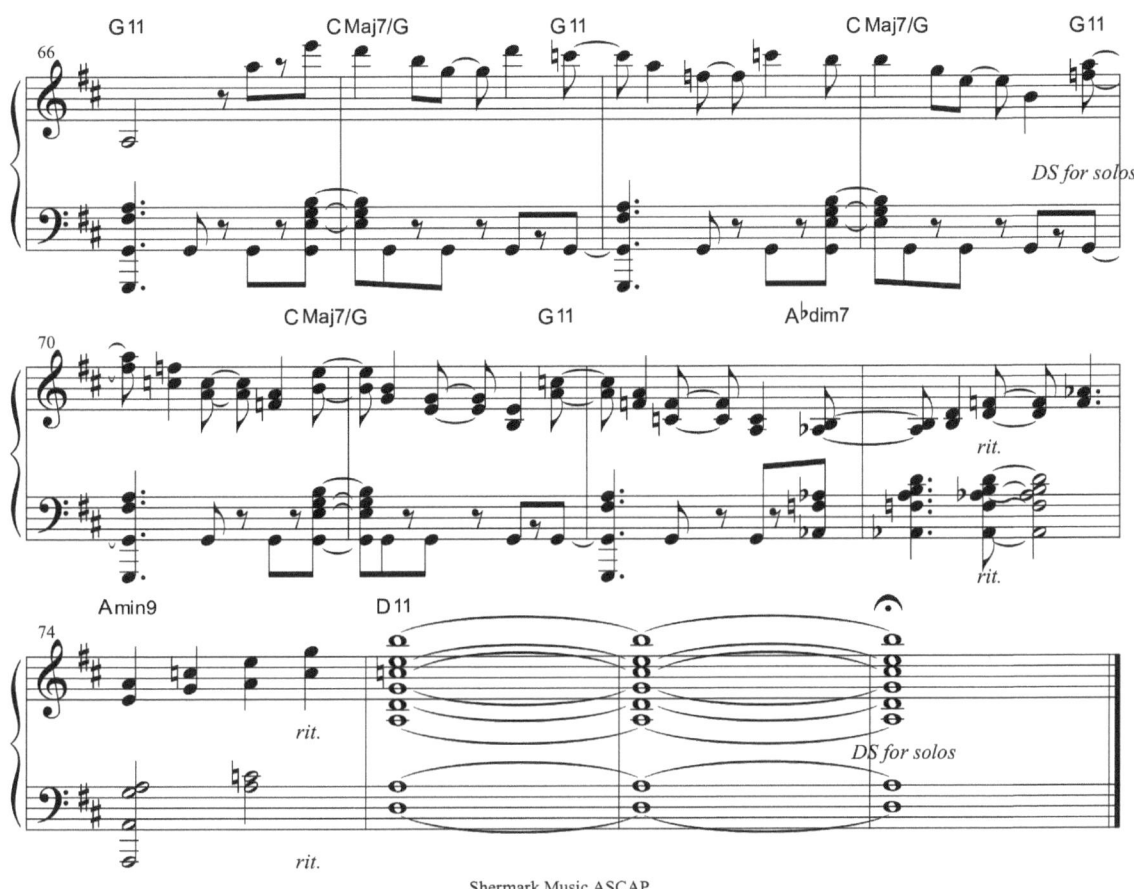

"The Music you are hearing is a culmination of my life study of the art of improvisation and the art of composition. The striving for the continuous study of sound and harmony brought to us from the great musical masters of our time. Coltrane, Stravinsky, McCoy, Elvin, Miles, Bags, Bird, Bartok, Rollins, and many others have planted the foundation for the music and it is up to my generation and the generations to come to continue to try to develop what has been left for us. … (Mark Sherman, December 2006)".

Explorations

Mark Sherman "Family First" MHR 8600 2006

Mark Sherman

Solos from letter A

Shermark Music ASCAP

Fantasize

"Family First" MHR 8600 2006

Mark Sherman

Straight eighth

Family First

"Family First" MHR 8606 2006

Mark Sherman

With Hope

"Family First" MHR 8600 2006

Mark Sherman

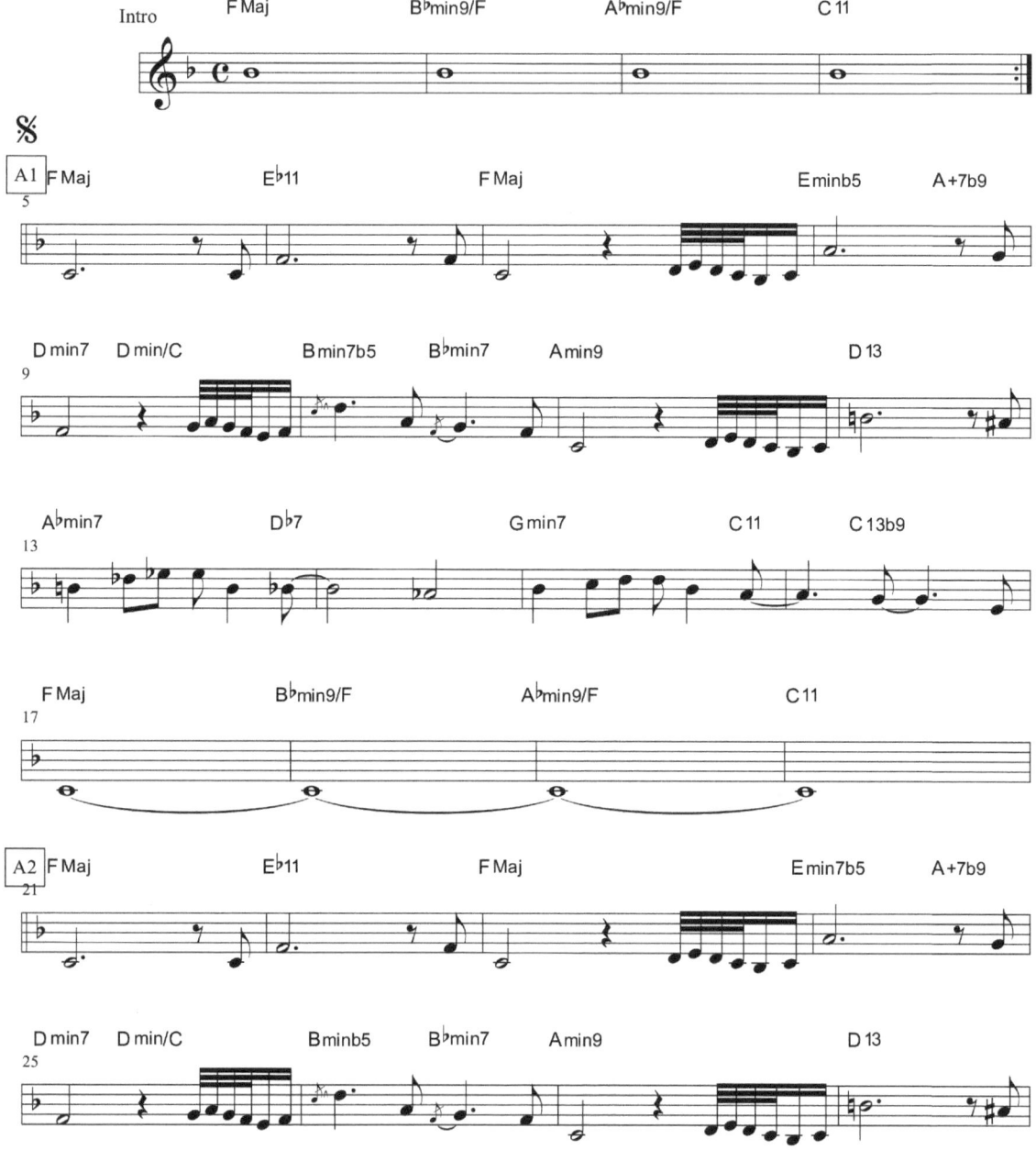

Symetrical

"Family First" MHR 8600 2006

Mark Sherman

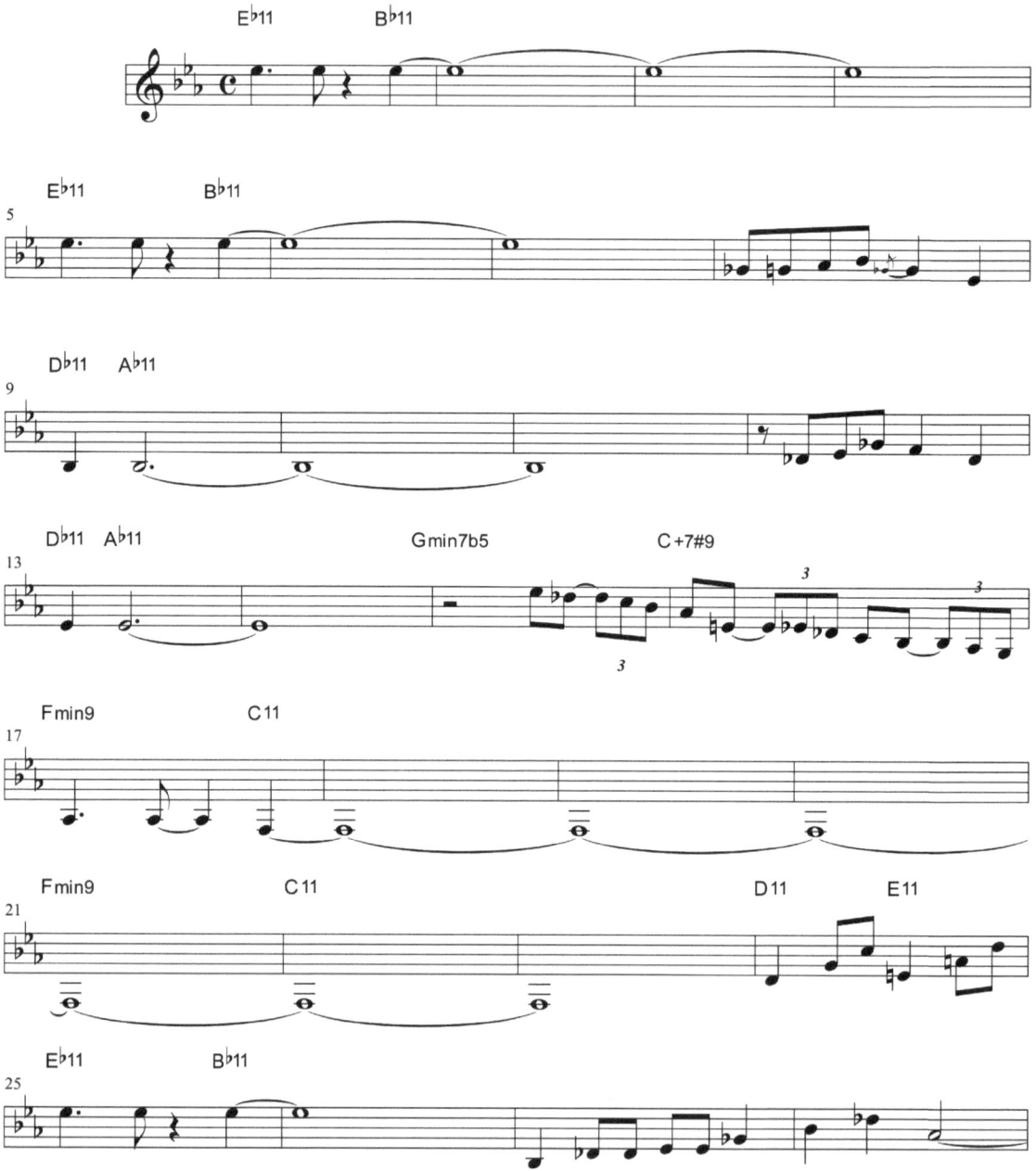

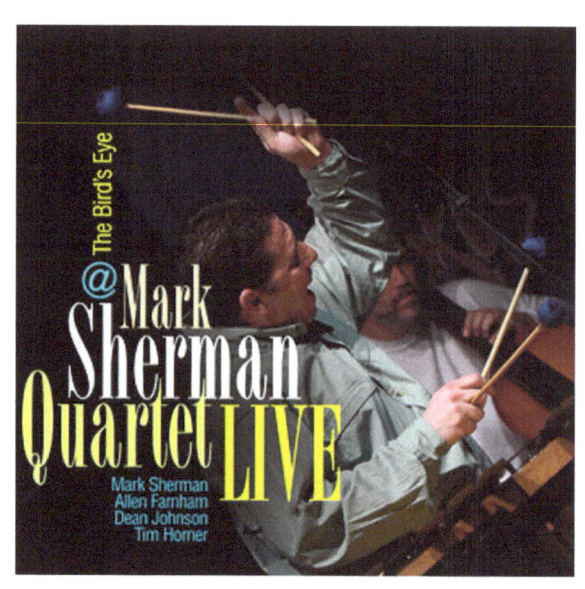

Tip Top Blues
"Live At The Bird's Eye" MHR 8606 2008

Mark Sherman

Shermark Music ASCAP Solos on Bb Blues

The Winning Life
"Live At The Bird's Eye" MHR 8606 2008

by Mark Sherman

Trust

"Live At The Bird's Eye" MHR 8606 2008

Mark Sherman

Tip Top Rhythm
"Live At The Bird's Eye" MHR 8606 2008

Mark Sherman

Shermark Music ASCAP

Hardship

"Live At The Bird's Eye" MHR 8606

Mark Sherman

Solos on form 2x's then F Blues

Shermark Music ASCAP

Hardship

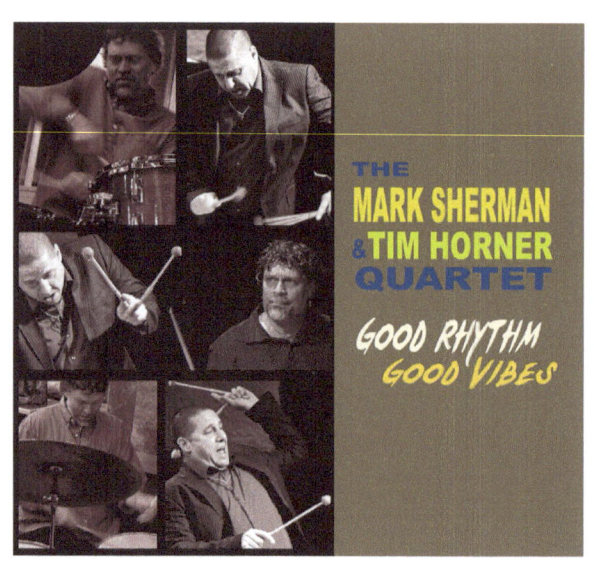

Sandy

Good Rhythm Good Vibes MHR 8611 2010

Mark Sherman

Gift For A Friend

Live @ Chorus Jazz Club

With Soul From Seoul
"Live At Chorus Jazz Club" MHR 8618 2011

Mark Sherman

Shermark Music ASCAP

81

Primitive Reality
"Live At Chorus Jazz Club" MHR 8618 2011

Mark Sherman

Primative Reality

Shermark Music ASCAP

Solitude
"Live At Chorus Jazz Club MHR 8618 2011

Mark Sherman

My Warm Heart

"Live At Chorus Jazz Club" MHR 8618 2011

Mark Sherman

My Warm Heart

Sherrmark Music ASCAP

Tree Of Life

"Live At Chorus Jazz Club" MHR 8618 2011

Mark Sherman

Tree Of Life

Tree Of Life

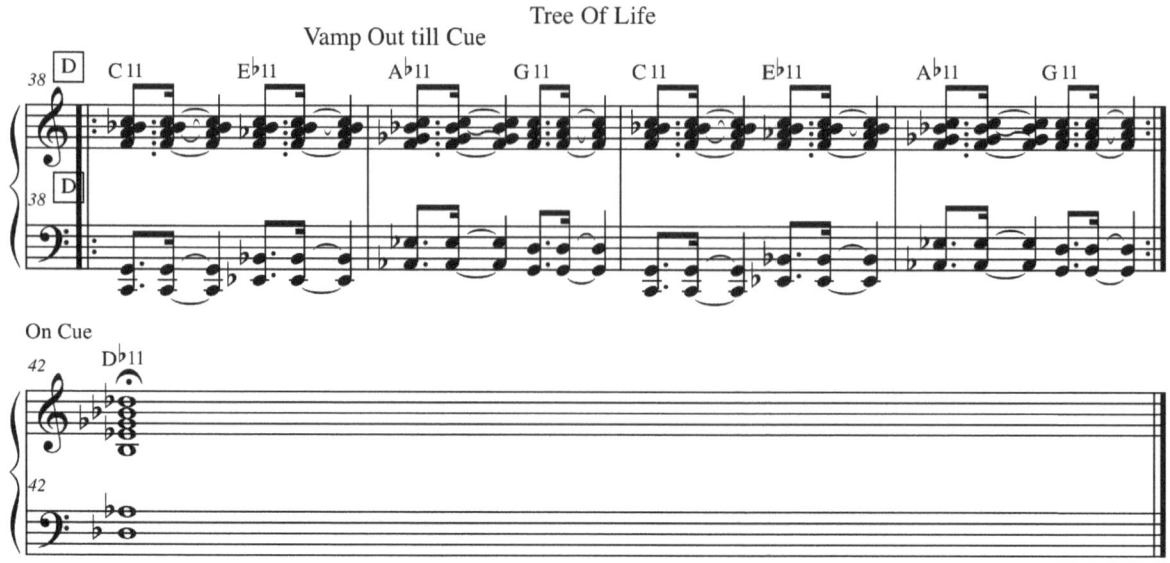

Shermark Music ASCAP

www.ingramcontent.com/pod-product-compliance
Lightning Source LLC
Chambersburg PA
CBHW042001150426
43194CB00002B/79